IMAGES OF WALES

UPPER RHONDDA
THE THIRD SELECTION

IMAGES OF WALES

UPPER RHONDDA
THE THIRD SELECTION

EMRYS JENKINS AND ROY GREEN

TEMPUS

Frontispiece: This book is dedicated to the memory of Roy Green, who sadly died in May during the production of this book.

First published 2006

Tempus Publishing Limited
The Mill, Brimscombe Port,
Stroud, Gloucestershire, GL5 2QG
www.tempus-publishing.com

British Library Cataloguing in Publication Data.
A catalogue record for this book is available from the British Library.

ISBN 0 7524 3784 4

Typesetting and origination by Tempus Publishing Limited.
Printed in Great Britain.

Contents

Acknowledgements

The authors wish to thank the following individuals and organisations for their considerable help in the compilation of this book. We are particularly indebted to Lyn Evans and Melinda Yeoman who have willingly opened their excellent photographic collections, thus allowing us to improve considerably our intended publication. We sincerely apologise to anyone who has helped over the years if they have been inadvertently omitted from the following list: Maureen and David Locke, Jill Evans, Derick Wilkins, Gwyn Evans, Hetty Harris, Danny Morgans, Emrys Richards, Terry Lewis, Jennie Lewis, Ralph Owen, Ron Pryce, Clive Thomas, Ann and Les Hill, Jo-ann Banner, Julie Spiller and the Penyrenglyn Project, Valley Kids Penygraig, Jeff and Eileen Long, Owen Morgan, better known by his bardic title 'Morien' author of *History of Pontypridd and Rhondda Valleys* published in 1903, *The Western Mail & Echo* and *The Rhondda Leader.* We would gratefully record our indebtedness to the many photographers whose work is featured in this book, some unknown and the following that have become synonymous with Rhondda: Stephen Timothy (Pentre), E. Lester (Treherbert), Marlin Norman (Pentre), Cyril Batstone (Pentre) and Ernest T. Bush.

Our special thanks go to the committee of Treherbert OAP Hall for the use of their hall, and last but not least to our wives Doreen Jenkins and Mavis Green for their patience and understanding and to Clive Thomas for his excellent introduction.

Introduction

In April of this year, Roy and Mavis came down to our home in Porthcawl and during our conversation he asked if I would be prepared to write the introduction of the new book. Beryl and I found him so enthusiastic and extremely dedicated to the Rhondda, that as a proud son of the valley, I felt it was a special honour to be asked to do this. We had left for holidays before I was able to give my copy to Roy and Emrys and unfortunately it was during our time in Portugal that we received the sad news of Roy's departure. We were absolutely shocked and couldn't believe that only a few weeks before we were enjoying his and Mavis's company at our home.

I hope, therefore, you understand that I have had to change certain parts of this introduction.

The incredible history of Upper Rhondda is fascinating for anyone with an interest in our industrial and social past, which was so well illustrated by Emrys Jenkins and Roy Green in the first publication in 1997.

I have nothing but praise for the diligent and dedicated work undertaken by Emrys and Roy whose names will live on for generations as the authors who have enabled us to cherish our roots through their documentation of Upper Rhondda life.

This valley played such crucial role in the shaping of modern Wales through the imagination of its engineers and the toil of those who worked underground. All of it would have been locked away in archives but for the work of the authors, to whom we owe a special dept of gratitude.

It's also incredible to reflect that the peak year for coal production in South Wales was 1913 – one year before the outbreak of the First World War. In that year alone, South Wales produced 54 million tonnes of coal, of which 13 million came from the Rhondda, mined by folk who came from many parts of Wales, the UK and many other parts of the globe.

Emrys and our late and dear friend Roy have captured all of this through their painstaking work. I hope that you as a reader will enjoy this new publication as much as I shall. If I could, I would award them both an FA Cup winners' medal. It's the very least they deserve!

Clive Thomas
2006

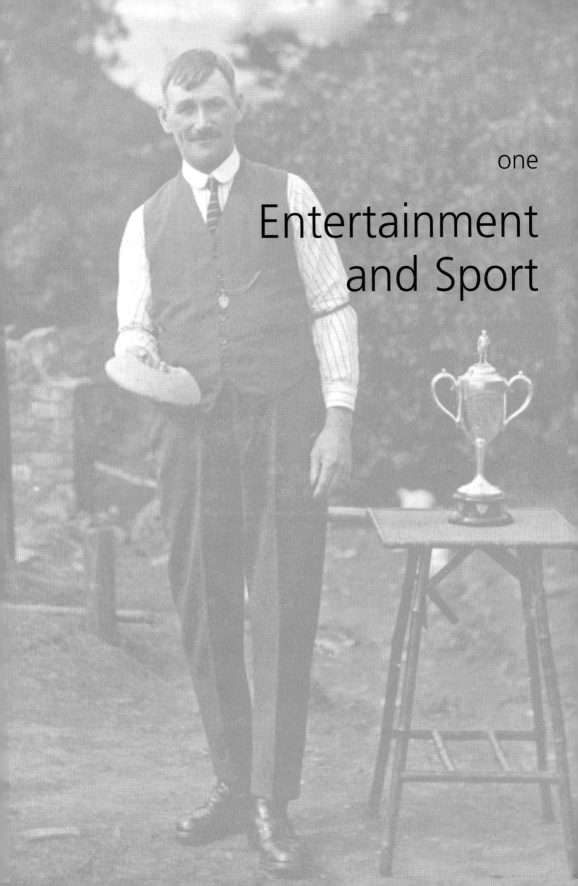

one

Entertainment and Sport

Selsig Operatic Society, *Waltz Dream*, 1981. From left to right: Mary Jones, Doreen Lee, Jayne Fletcher.

Selsig Operatic Society, *Waltz Dream*, 1981. Men's chorus from left to right: Glyn Holmes, John Phelps, Mel Parfit, Roy Duncan, Harry Corfield, Graham Jones, -?-, Gwyn Davies, Tom Cullen, Mel Davies. Seated: Alan Rossiter, Brian Hall, Aldyth Jones.

Above left: Selsig Operatic Society, *Waltz Dream*, 1981. From left to right: Megan Davies, Harry Corfield, Barrie Hall, Jean Phelps.

Above right: Selsig Operatic Society, ballet dancers' performance of *Valley of Song*, 1975. Back row, Jayne Fletcher. Second row, from left to right: Jayne Daniels, Vicki Jones. Front row: Lisa Holmes, Angela Beddoe.

Selsig Operatic Society, *Land of Smiles*, 1973. Back row, from left to right: Kevin Morgan, Marian Davies, Kevin Ralley. Seated left Linda Pritchard, seated right Beti Edwards.

Left: Selsig Operatic Society, *Magyar Melody*, 1977. Back row, from left to right: Betty Evans, John Beddoe, Lil Evans. Front row: Judith Gunt, Betty Hater, Cath Davies.

Below: Selsig Operatic Society, *Waltz Dream*, 1981. Back row, from left to right: -?-, Trevor Locke, Gwyn Davies, D. Morgan, Tom Phelps, Johnny Edmunds, John Phelps, Howard Hughes, Graham Jones, Tom Cullen. Seated: Mel Davies, Glyn Holmes. In front: Alan Rossiter, Alan Miller.

Above: Selsig Operatic Society
performance of the *Gondoliers*, 1974.
From left to right: John Elwyn Jones,
Aldyth Jones, Maureen Fletcher,
Ray Daniels.

Right: Selsig Operatic Society, *Waltz
Dream*, 1981. Back row, from left to right:
May Purdell, Margaret Evans, Betty Evans,
May Evans, Marion John. Front row:
Cath Davies, Beti Edwards, N. Richards.

Selsig Operatic Society celebration evening with CISWO cup for performance of *Valley of Song*, 1975.

Above left: Selsig Operatic Society, *Land of Smiles*, 1973. From left to right: Tom Cullen, Myra Thomas, Gethin Jones.

Above right: Selsig Operatic society, *Waltz Dream*, 1981. From left to right: Marlene Evans, Mel Davies, Glyn Holmes, Cath Davies.

Above left: Selsig Operatic Society, *Waltz Dream*, 1981. From left to right: Lyn Evans, Betty Evans.

Above right: Selsig Operatic Society, *Land of Smiles*, 1973. From left to right: Marian Davies, Beti Edwards.

Selsig Operatic Society CISWO winners for the performance of *Valley of Song*, 1975. From left to right: Eifion Evans MD, Stella Willey accompanist, John Beddoe producer.

Above: Performance of *Ali Baba* by members of Wesleyan chapel, *c.* 1935. The men are Jim Phelps (back) and Arthur Phelps (front).

Left: Des Rees (cabaret stage name Danny Reason), vocalist at a charity show in Treherbert Boys Club. His motto was, 'To Please is my Pleasure'.

Opposite above, left: Opera House staff, *c.* 1912. Manager Mr D. Gwillim is on the left.

Opposite above, right: Opera House performer in *Trial by Jury, c.* 1912.

Opposite below: Selsig Operatic Society performance in the Tynewydd Workmans Hall (the Palace) of *The Bartered Bride*, 1955.

Rhondda Nightlife Concert Party, 1940, who entertained under the auspices of ENSA during the war years. This enabled them to get petrol coupons which allowed them to travel to various venues. Back row, from left to right: -?- Basini, Gladys Jenkins, Emrys Richards, -?- Granville. Front row: Bel Roy (Cyril Jones), Ron Holley.

Opposite above: The Tynewydd Hotel (The Bricks) Darts Team, *c.* 1952. Back row, from left to right: Emrys Warren, Glyn Evans, Ernie Taylor, Walt Chick, Llew Evans, Jack Thomas, Cyril Dando, Alwyn Evans. Front row: Russell Howells, Rosie Nash, Eddy Phillips, Fred Harris, Evan Evans, Anna Bowen. Anna Bowen was the landlady of the hotel assisted by her sister, Rosie.

Opposite below: Gelli Linnets cricket team, *c.* 1926.

Ystrad Keep Fit ladies team. Back row, from left to right: Ivy Baldwin, Rosa Davies, Minnie Fisher, Mrs Thomas, Mrs Williamson, Gladys Sheppard (teacher), Hida Baker, Florrie Derrik, Bessie Heath, Mrs Moses (peeping), Mrs Griffiths, Gladys Jones, Martha Macnally. Middle row: Gwen Hall, Edith Reeves, Morfydd Knight, Gladys Collins, Eunice Williams, Mrs Stobart, Mary Almond, Dilys Candy. Front row: Gwen Vokes, Dolly Penetta, Vi Hall, -?- Pearce, Jenny Walby, Annie Candy, -?- Phillips, Mrs Cooper, Doll Sheppard, Mrs Green, Mrs Cochlin, Doris Vergo.

Treherbert AFC, 1913-14.

Treorchy Comprehensive School Rugby Team, 1949-50. Back row, from left to right: Clive Thomas, Brian Merriman, John Loney, Fred Lewis. Second row: Malcolm Lawther, Ken Tompkinson, Malcolm Evans, Maldwyn Barfoot, Cliff Trott, John Pearce. Front row: Percy Griffiths (headmaster), John Isaacs, -?-, John Birmingham, Colin Evans, Elwyn Williams, Haydn Williams (teacher).

Dunraven School Football Team, 1973. Back row, from left to right: Ron Jones (headmaster), Mark Richards, Paul Butcher, Wesley Collins, David -?-, Chris Cook, John Davies, Paul Evans, Stephen Richards, Mr Edwards (teacher). Middle row: Paul Davies, Wayne Warren, Alun Jones, Alan Hall, Stephen Edwards. Front row: Keith Ware, Alan Rees, Martin Jones, -?-Chambers, Ian Lewis.

Above: Treorchy Boys Club, season 1953. They were under-16s winners of all competitions in the Upper Rhondda League. Back row, from left to right: Tom Grant (trainer), Dennis Rose, Arwel Morgan, John Jones, Len Davies, Ken Scane, Lyn Clarke (secretary). Front row: Tony Rees, Clive Thomas, David Parry, Gwyn Evans, Gareth Evans, David Herbert, Ken Matthews. They were winners of two cups, Vaughan and Knockout, and one shield as League Champions.

Above: Penyrenglyn Juniors Touch Rugby Team Year 6, winners of the Rhondda Shield 2005. Back row, from left to right: Sadie Bebb, Adam Vaughan, Tyrone Terrell, Dean -?-, Leon Morris, Byron Jones, Rhys Morris. Front row: Wesley Owen, Camillo Strinati, Josh Ducket (captain), Lee Owen, Steffan Oliver.

Right: Fred Yeoman, quoits champion, played for the Baglan Hotel, Penyrenglyn.

Opposite below: Treherbert Juniors AFC, 1935–36. Back row, from left to right: Charlie Thomas, -?-, -?-, Dai Morris, Eddie Gough, Cyril John, Dai Sheriden, Ben Dando, Eddie Smart, -?-. Middle row: Gwyn Davies, Danny Fitzgerald, -?-, Will Jenkins, Ernie Greedy. Front row: Dai Howells, John Pearce. Apparently they all got drunk after the event and lost half the cups.

Cory Band, 1979. Denzil Stephens is the conductor.

Members of cornet section of the Cory Band, 1979. From left to right: Jim Davies, Ralph Morgan, John Neathy, Richard Dix.

Cwmparc Gondoliers Jazz Band, 1926.

Glenrhondda Silver Band. Bandmaster F. Prior, on his right T. Thomas, chairman, and left, H. Lewis Scott, secretary. They were SW & BBA Cup winners, Abertridwr and Championship Shield winners, Pontypridd 1949.

Above: Jonney Gowan heads the Toy Drum Majors Jazz Band, marching through Station Street, Treherbert.

Above: Moirwyn Williams Legionaire Dance Band, *c.* 1950. Back row, from left to right: Evan Jones, Ted Gough, Glan Williams, Roy Williams. Front Row: Haydn Brazel, Ron Lewis, Moirwyn Williams, John Jones, Ossie Harris.

Right: Poster advertising a dance held in Polikoffs canteen, April 1946.

Opposite below: Freda Watts leads the Green & White Crescents Jazz Band marching through Dunraven Street, Treherbert.

POLIKOFF'S ASSEMBLY ROOMS

A GRAND OLD ENGLISH

BALL

(Under the auspices of the Treherbert Hospital Canine Society)

Easter Monday, April 22, 1946

Dance to the Music of a Brand New Orchestra

THE LEGIONAIRES

Directed by Mr. MOIRWYN WILLIAMS.

M.C.: Mr. TOM POWELL

Tickets---2s.6d.

REFRESHMENTS at Moderate Prices.   DANCING 7.30 to 12.   LATE BUSES

Proceeds to be the First Shot at a Target of £1,200 needed for

A NEW X-RAY APPARATUS FOR TREHERBERT HOSPITAL

Members of Parc & Dare Band; Will Williams largest bandsman and largest instrument double. B. and Ernie Coombs smallest bandsman and smallest instrument cornet, around 1936.

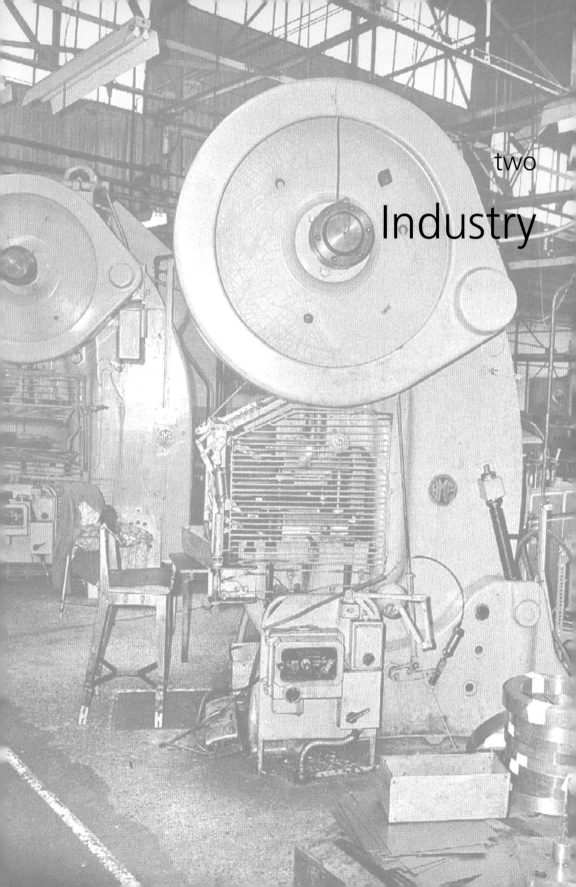

two

Industry

Above: Fernhill Colliery NUM Lodge officials, 1972. From left to right: Cliff True, Lou Evans (not an official), George Rees, Don Bundock, Harry Pearce.

Left: Hitchers & Hauliers Park Colliery, Cwmparc, July 1923.

Above: Group of colliers from Maendy Colliery. Second from the left is Edgar Jones.

Below: Bodringallt Colliery, Ystrad, *c.* 1910.

Prince Phillip and colliery officials descending the pit on a visit to Fernhill Colliery, 28 April 1955.

Opposite above: Abergorchy Colliery, Treorchy, *c.* 1905. Note the wooden headgear on the shafts.

Opposite below: Bute Colliery, Treherbert, *c.* 1928.

Abergorky Colliery, Treorchy.

Gwyn Morgan recording GPO dial life tests, EMI factory.

Evan Evans operating the press and shear machine, EMI factory.

EMI machine shop. From left to right: production engineer Gordon Richards and estimator Alan Tapper checking production times on the automatic press.

EMI engineering dept, *c.* 1975. Back row, from left to right; Gwyn Morgan, Ken Stoneman, Chris Morris, Ian Williams, -?-, Bill Cooksey, John Stevens, Maureen McGovern, Terry Hartnoll, Gordon Richards, Cyril Brooks, Roger Mitchell, -?-, Horace Burge, Alan Tapper. Front row: Ron Pryce, Roy Bowen, Dave Tomlinson, Ralph Owen.

Above: EMI managers. From left to right: Derick Wilkins, Bill Burgess, Clive Lewis, Dave Evans, Jim Stephenson, J. -?-, Jim Barnes.

Left: EMI machine shop, 50-ton presses. These were brought down to Treorchy from the parent factory at Hayes, Middlesex in 1945.

EMI plating shop. Danny Phillips.

EMI; Mark Jones checking printed circuit boards after passing through the flow solder machine.

Rollo (Stelco) Hardy factory, May 1983.

Cutting room at Polikoffs.

Injection moulding machine, Valdon Plastics, Treorchy.

Polikoffs factory despatch dept, eyes front for the photographer, around Christmas time, 1945.

Visit of recording star and dance band leader, Joe Loss, to EMI on Friday 7 October 1977. From left to right: -?-, Clive Lewis, Joe Loss, Jim Stevenson, Bernard McGrath, Derick Wilkins, Dave Evans.
Joe travelled to Treorchy by train but unfortunately fell asleep and woke up in Aberavon. Lunch was delayed as the company had to send a car to pick him up and return to Treorchy.

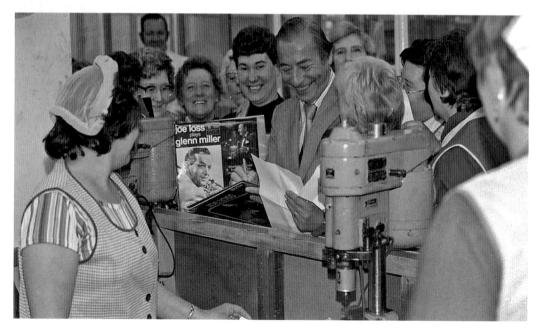

Joe Loss signs autographs for the machine shop girls on his visit to EMI .

Production line EMI factory, c. 1966.

EMI products on exhibition, April 1958.

Polifoffs factory workers, c. 1975.

Polikoff girls' Christmas party, c.1960. Back row, from left to right: Jean Farley, Hilda Collins, Katy Watkins, Silvy Drew, Hetty Harris, -?-, Grace Davies. Front row: Doreen Stanton, Jean Morris, Muriel Lewis, Margie Lome, -?-, Lynda Mathews.

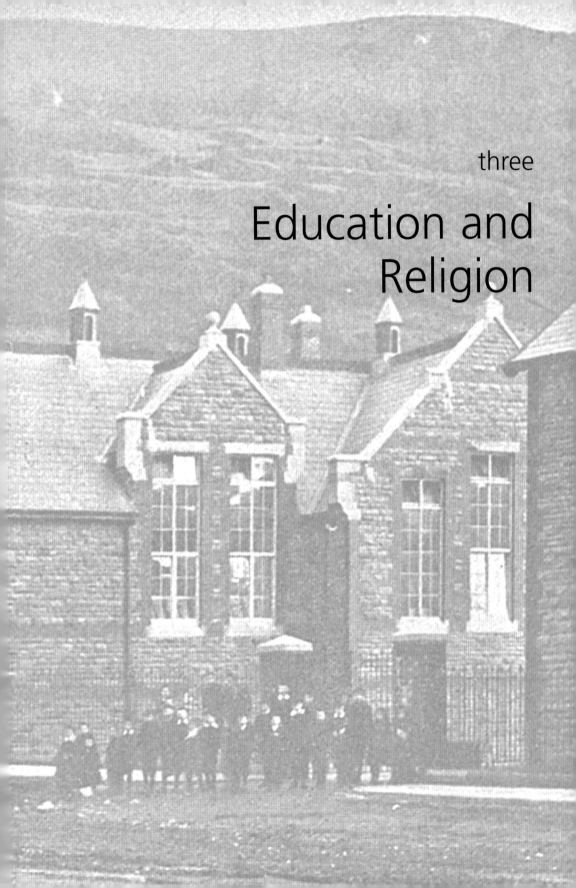

three

Education and Religion

Staff at Bodringallt Senior School, 1975. Back row, from left to right: Peter Jones, (music and PE), David Jones (RI), Vernon Jones, (woodwork), Mr Jones (English), Mrs Williams (cookery), Kay Almond (secretary), Elizabeth Davies (Welsh and geography). Front row: Tom Jones (art), Idris Evans (Sach) (science), Gwyn Jones (headmaster), Sheila Taylor (PE), Miss Gould (needlework).

Bodringallt Infant School, c. 1959-60. Back row, from left to right: Marrisa Coppola, John Willis, David Edwards, David Coleman, Anthony Kinsey, John Simmonds, -?-, -?-, Peter Katanowic, Wayne Walker, Geraldine Lewis, Yvonne Sealey. Middle row: Mary Galliger, Elizabeth -?-, Mary Bayliss, Teressa Virga, Marilyn Matthews, Marion Powell, Sally Richards, -?-, Coral Pearce, -?- , Jaquline Barretta. Front row: Vicky Wigsel, Cheryl Ashman, Michelle Williams, Elaine Turner, Jeanette Old, Patricia Perry, Marilyn Price, Beryl Hawkins (teacher). On the right is Mrs Terry.

Cwmparc Infants School, 1960.

Blaenrhondda School Sports, 1935.

Dunraven School, 1936.

Cwmparc babies, 1961.

Bodringallt School, Ystrad.

Class 6, Bodringallt School, 1956-57. Back row, from left to right: Mrs Williams (headmistress), Brian Mayhew, Jeffrey Belmont, Michael Williams, David Griffiths, David Jones, James Harrod, Michael Williams, Paul Evans, Harry Applin, Gerald Williams, Stephen Lewis, Geraint Draper, Robert Abraham Thomas, Mrs George (teacher). Middle row: Margaret Bumford, Jean Eagan, Mary Tutton, June Rees, Paula Lewis, Linda Davies, Elaine Morgan, Josephine Phillips, Anna Davies, Gillian Brabbon, Glynis Jones, Janet Williams. Front row: Kieth Prichard, Leonard Shurey, Brian Winter, Mair Lewis, Pauline Haskins, Anita Hughes, Gary Thomas, Kevin Ellis, Frank Coppolo.

Above: Penyrenglyn Infants School, 1961. Back row, from left to right: Colin Jones, Raymond Barnes, Antony Brunker, Terry Lewis, John Jones, Malcolm Fisher. Third row: Steven James, Mark Stephens, Julie Perkins, David Todd Jones, Christopher Todd Jones, Denise Collins, Phillip Evans, Kim James. Second row: Julie Davies, Glyn Probert, Georgina Parcell, Graham Vickery, Margaret Davies, Ian Richards, Christine Parsons, John Smart. Front row: Patricia Hill, Joan Powell, Wendy Davies, Helen Jones, Linda Edwards, Carol Samuel.

Parc Girls School, standard 5, 1936. Included in the photograph are: Pat Townsend, Pheoni Tortello, Miss Sadie Davies (teacher), Betty Clayton.

Above: Pentre Primary School, 1947–48.

Opposite below: Dunraven School, 1936. Back row, from left to right: Charlie Goodman, Elwyn Richards, -?-, Howard Biggs, Jeffrey Gilbert, Ivory Vaughan, -?-, Jimmy Squires. Second row: Billy Farmer, Ivy Hunt, -?-, Peg Sperry, -?-, Thalami James, -?-, -?-, -?-. Third row: Megan Harris, Marjorie Kinsey, Mary Williams, Rona Rees, Jessie Doughty, -?-, Marion Jones, Muriel Guy, Ruby Chitty, -?-, Miss Jones (teacher). Front row: Roy Davies, Cliff Morgan, Fred Thomas, Gordon Evans, Idwal Wallace, -?-, -?-.

Parc Girls School, standard 4a, 1931. The teacher is Olwen Edwards who was also the conductress of Polikoffs Girls' Choir.

Above: Dunraven School, 1926.

Opposite above: Treherbert Boys School, form 2a, May 1962. Back row, from left to right: Tony James, Phil Harris, Gwyn Jenkins, Jas Francis, Stuart Thomas, Len Samuel, Gwyn Rees, Phil Thomas, -?-. Middle row: Alan Thomas, Dennis Jones, Ray Mees, Mike Ducket, Roger Streeter, Mike Protheroe, Kevin Ralley, Ivor Mace. Front row: Mr David Parry, Barry Jones, Ron Marsh, Mike Pugh, Keith Melyn, Alan Bishop, Mr D. Gwyn Davies.

Opposite below: Treherbert Boys School, form 2a, 1960. Back row, from left to right: Gary Thomas, John Gough, Keryl Colwille, Alan Davies, Howard Griffiths, Malcolm Jones, Graham Green, -?-. Middle row: Ken Deane, Alun Jenkins, Leighton Rich, John Owen, Alun Clemas, Gwynfor Williams, Henry Bates. Front row: Idris Thomas, David Lewis, John Payne, Phillip Jones, Phillip Morgan, Michael Jenkins, Phillip Jenkins.

Penyrenglyn Infant School on fire, 12.30 p.m., 8 March 2004.

Penyrenglyn Infant School on fire, 12.30 p.m., 8 March 2004.

Penyrenglyn School after demolition of the Infant School, March 2004.

Start of the demolition of Penyrenglyn Junior School, April 2004.

Above: Bodringallt School, 1955. Back row, from left to right: Stephen Lewis, Jeffrey Beams, Michael Williams, Glynis Jones, Yvonne Harris, Maureen Griffiths, Diane Nash, Carol Thomas. Middle row: Gary Thomas, Paul Lewis, Margaret Leonard, Linda Davies, Josephine Phillips, Janet James, Gillian Brabbon, Jeffrey Belmont, Frank Coppola. Front row: Harry Alpin, Ceryl Jenkins, Kevin Andrews, Geraint Draper, Phillip Williams, Gerald Williams, Jean Eagan, Derek Morgan, Raymond Baker, Anna Davies.

Below: Bodringallt Junior School, Ystrad, 1951-52. Back row, from left to right: Mr Owen (headmaster), Gary Bennett, Brian Fowler, Colin Fletcher, Ronald Flynn, Joan Berry, Diane Harris, Pat Collins, Maurice Griffiths, Donald Davies, Tony Jones, Stuart White. Middle row: Alan Upshall, Alan Roe, Robert Young, Ieuan Davies, Janice Hannam, Ann Jones, Christine Davies, David Cowley, Ken Baldwin, Clive Collins, Phillip Cowley, Mrs Evans (teacher). Front row: Brian Edwards, Gillian Jenkins, Marlise Lewis, Maureen Tucker, -?-, Joyce James, Pat Morris, Mair Lewis, Joan Jacobs, Jill Weaver, Maldwyn Davies.

Above: Penyrenglyn Junior School, standard 4, *c.* 1975. Back row, from left to right: Andrew Williams, Andrew Webb, Adrian –?–, Darren Williams, –?–, Andrew Tynan, Phillip Walters, Vivian Jones, Christopher Searle. Third row: Colin Deanes, –?–, Paul Coleman, Lynwen Jenkins, Siân Rees, Jacquline Jones, Vincent Chambers, Kevin Davies, Darren Rees, Mrs Handcock. Second row: Gaynor Jones, Michelle Collins, Lisa Morgan, Janette Middleton, Debbie Wilde, Natalie Wade, Pamela Warren, Yvette Davies, Katherine Merry. Front row: John Clarke, –?–, –?–, Paul Clement, Gerry Hughes, Nicholas –?–, –?–, –?–.

Below: New School, Treorchy.

Elim chapel, Ystrad, *c.* 1950. Back row, from left to right: Edith Jones, Grace Griffiths, Ivy Vergo, Mrs Derrik, Blod Davies, Maggie Dee, Lizzie May Thomas, Valmi Davies, Rita Lewis, Maggie Morris, June Todd, Iris Green, Oenwen Jones. Second row: Mrs Rees holding Vicky Kear, Mrs Daily, Maureen Kelly, Lyn Jacobs, Gloria Williams, Sheila Watkins, Joan Jacobs, Jaqualine Thomas, Valerie Green, Barbara Nash, Maralyn Davies, Marina Morris, Carol Wright, Bessie Todd, Phyllis Rowlands, little boy –?–, Mrs Kelly. Third row: little girl –?–. Annie Cross, Mrs Williams, Maggie Williams, Janet Cross, Marilyn Kear, Gillian Jenkins, Joyce Thomas, Mair Lewis, Brenda Coates, Pat Tipple, –?–. Front row: Mrs Collins, Mrs Gilbert, Alan Jones, Rosalyn Gilbert, Mr Gilbert, Christine Vergo, Lynette Jenkins, –?–, Gillian Morgan, Marilyn Wrought, Betty Kelly, Mair Griffiths, Gosta Davies, Pastor Jones, Mrs Roberts, Miss Sage. Front: boy on left kneeling, Ronald Green; boy in middle sitting, Michael Kelly; boy on right kneeling, John Marshman.

Providence chapel, Ystrad, Sisterhood Group's annual outing.

Beulah chapel undergoing demolition, High Street, Treorchy.

Carmel Dramatic Society, Treherbert, performance of *Corlan Y Pentref*, February 1939. Standing, from left to right: Mr Henry, Mr D.C. Edwards, –?–, Mrs Watkins (insurance), –?–, Will Kinsey, Mr Watkins, May Thomas (Butch), –?–, –?–. Seated: Lizzie Parry, Bob Evans, –?–, Glan Davies.

The Foundation stone, 1985.

John Poole Hughes, Bishop of Llandaff, conducting the service during the stone-laying of St John's church, 6 July 1985.

Deacons and minister of Blaencwm chapel, Tynewydd. Back row, from left to right: Gwilym Lloyd, G. Edwards, John Rees, Dafydd Morgan (Delicious), Ben Thomas. Front row: Alfred Evans, W.R. Morgan, D. Thomas, W. Cynon-Evans (minister), W. Thomas (butcher), T. Lawrence.

Blaencwm chapel Sunday School class around 1935. Back row, from left to right: Mrs Williams (Gadlys), -?-, Mrs. Williams (Will Henry), Mrs Sarah Owen (Miskin St), Mrs Griffiths (Tommey Siapwr), Mrs Blod Price, -?-. Middle row: Mrs Trevor Price, Mrs Morgan (first), Mrs Lucy Davies, Mrs Grinstead, Mrs Uriel Williams, Mrs Williams, Mrs Hicks (Glyngwyn). Front row: Mrs Bonner (baker), -?-, Mrs Lawrence, Mr Tommy Lawrence, Mrs Thomas (butcher), Miss Nicholas.

Dunraven Junior School, 1956–57. Back row, from left to right: –?–, Huw Jones, Idris Thomas, Robert Daniels, Keryl Colwille, Robert Jones, Derek or Denzil Davies, Nigel Mortimer, Howard Jones, –?–. Second row: Mr Butler (teacher), Vivian Griffiths, Ronald Marsh, Shirley Jones, Paul Woolfe, David Thomas, Mr Williams (headmaster). Third row: Diane Wigley, Christine Doughty, Lucy Cook, Gillian Smart, Pauline Davies, Anita Davies, Pat Phelps, Marilyn Andrews, Wendy Nash, Maureen Gough, Cheryl Langley. Front row: Alun Lewis, Keith Howells, Keryl John, Dorian Davies, David Lewis.

Above: Penyrenglyn Infant School, 1913. The two boys on the right in the front row are Dickie and Cliff Crabbe.

Opposite below: Teacher Don Fenwick Williams supervising boys' playtime, on he stone field situated in front of Treherbert Girls' School is in the background.

Above: Cwmparc Juniors, 1964–65.

Treherbert Board National School, 19 July 1900. Best and most regular.

National School Penyrenglyn started in 1861. Headmaster Mr J. Pollard was paid £1 per week. Pupils' ages were eight to eighteen years. They called it the 'Penny School' as each child had to pay one penny per day for upkeep.

four

Events

Above left: First World War carnival group, *c.* 1916.

Above right: Megan Allen dressed as a pearly queen and Jinney Lewis as a toff, Queen Elizabeth's Silver Jubilee, 1977.

Queen Elizabeth II's Silver Jubilee, 1977. All girls together from left to right: John Oliver, Phillip Jones, Don Tegan, Ken Eynon, Gwyn Taylor, Mike Rees, with John Gowan in front.

Rhondda Mayor John Davies with the sheriff of Western World passing the Baglan Hotel on their way to the opening day on the Fernhill site.

The Texans are coming to Western World, 1987.

Cliff Richard and Keith Doughty of Tynewydd in Cliff's 'E' type Jaguar car, *c.* 1963. Keith met Cliff in Blackpool when he parked his 'E' type Jaguar next to his in a car park near the Winter Gardens where Cliff was performing. They became firm friends, and it was not unusual to see Cliff driving through the Rhondda to visit Keith and his family in Tynewydd. Keith was employed by Cliff as a chef in his Winchester restaurant between 1979-1983.

Cliff Richard and Keith Doughty in the London Palladium where Keith presented him with a klaxon which he had specially chrome plated for his 'E' type Jaguar.

Ladies of the Women's Voluntary Services outside St Peter's church, Pentre, 1945. The men are: left Mr E.D. Wilde (deputy clerk RUDC); right Mr D.J. Jones, (clerk Rhondda Urban District Council).

Parade celebrating the Relief of Mafeking, passing the Singer Sewing Machine Co. Ltd, at No. 228 Ystrad Road, Pentre, May 1900. Note the letter 'S' on the wall, top centre on the photograph.

Pentre drinking fountain is a memorial to the late Mr W.H. Llewellyn, a partner of the firm of Llewellyn & Cubitt Engineers, Rhondda Engine Works of Pentre. Mr Llewellyn's sudden death took place on the night of 12 April 1877 when he fell over a high wall, near Park Pit, on his way home from the Ogmore Valley.

Right: Dr Min Tin enjoys a pint of beer outside the bar of Tydraw Farm Riding School, 1979.

Below: Stone and rubbish washed down from the mountain and piled against Reginald Howells's shop at No. 3 Scott Street, Tynewydd, after the floods on 6 July 1939. In the doorway are Reginald Howells and his son Russell. The dog's name was Terry. Some of the goods in the shop window are: Oxo, champion for cup or cooking, Stork margarine, Condor twist, Oxydol soap powder, Sylvan soap, Imp soap and washer, Eve shampoo, Pearce Duff's jellies, Saxa salt, Saxa pepper, Colman's mustard, Haza tomato sauce, Carters liver salt, HP sauce, health salts, Sylvan soap flakes, Will's flake tobacco, McVitie and Price biscuits.

HRH the Prince of Wales visits Penyrenglyn Community Project, 29 July 2003. Julie Spiller looks on as he talks to the children.

Prince Charles shakes hands with Artist Hamza at Penyrenglyn Centre, 29 July 2003.

Betty Price of No. 74 Eileen Place, Tynewydd, became the first Treherbert hospital queen at the age of thirteen years on 14 June 1928.

Tydraw Farm Riding School cavalcade. A horse and carriage is passing St Matthew's church, Treorchy, 1979.

Clive Thomas with Speaker of the House, George Thomas, Lord Tonypandy, at Westminster in 1972.

Fernhill Presentation, 1977–78. Back row, from left to right: Cliff True, Fred Griffiths, Brian Richards, Ianto Smith, Keith Barnes, Willie Davies (Pharo), -?-, Don Bundock. Second row: Eifron Bowen, Tom Worral, Phil Rees, -?-, Will Green, Len Smith, Tommy Harris, -?-. Front row: Bennt Rees (Baish), Will Davies (Buster), Alby Oliver, Trevor Lewis, Ivy Phipps (canteen lady), Mr Thomas, Albert Sealey, Ken Carrol, Chris Phillips.

Herbert Street outing to Blackpool, *c.* 1950. Back row, from left to right row: Margie Pyer, Arthur Jones, George Fisher, Glyn Jones, -?-, Johnie Pyer, Johnie Rupe Jones. Second row: Eunice Fisher, Myra Oliver, Doreen Jones, Lizzy Fisher, Betty Tanner, -?- Jones. Front row: Alby Oliver, Charlie Fisher, Gwilym Tanner.

Above: Mike Rees dressed as a native warrior for Herbert Street Carnival.

Opposite above: On the left is Roy Paul, famous Welsh international footballer with right, Clive Thomas, famous football referee. In the background between Roy and Clive is Wynford Ludlow.

Opposite below: Albert Nicholas (Alby Nick) and Clive Thomas at the official publication of Clive's book *By the Book* about football referees.

Lord Brecon being presented to actor Stanley Baker with Clive and Beryl Thomas in attendance, date unknown.

Clive Thomas and singer Frankie Vaughan on their visit to Treherbert Boys Club, October 1968.

Wales rugby coach Graham Henry signs his autograph for Joanne Morris on the Welsh International Team's visit to Penyrenglyn Community Project in 2000.

Welsh international rugby player Neil Jenkins with his adoring fans during a team visit to Penyrenglyn Community Project in 2000.

Compressor boiler on the Rhigos Mountain, being transported to the reservoir.

Horses pulling equipment on the Rhigos Mountain for use by the reservoir.

five

Organisations

UTG 646G

Bodringallt Youth Club Choir, *c.* 1947.

St John's Ambulance Brigade presentation to cadet of the year, Amanda Durbin. From left to right: Stephen Durbin, Malcolm Durbin, Gemma Harris, Ester Harris, Amanda Durbin, Christine Durbin, Helen Arundel standing in front of Christine, David Harris. The little girl in front is Kerry Arundel.

Treorchy Male Voice Choir's visit to Switzerland, September 1963. Members of the choir pose for the photographer near Mount Pilatus with the funicular cars in the background. Dai Griffiths, far left, is rushing to get in on the act. The visit was sponsored by the National Coal Board.

Girl Guides first aid drill, *c.* 1935.

Members of Treherbert Gardening Society, 1997–80. Back row, from left to right: Roy Green, Gerald Rose, Keith Barnes, Jack Spury, John Creedy, Maxie James, Keith Addis. Second row: John Ellis, Alan Jones, Harry Corfield, David Jones, David Snell, Alan Pickens, Emrys Jenkins, Betty Harris. Front row: June Ellis, Marianne Jones, Rose Corfield, Renie Aldridge, Ethel Spury, Maureen Carpenter, Melinda Yeoman, Pat Chambers.

Bodringallt LEA Centre, winners of the Youth Drama Festival, 1947, with *The Story of Ruth*. In the photograph are Audrey Almond and Rita Gosling.

Treherbert Hospital Nursing Staff, June 1948. Back row, from left to right: Maureen Woods (probationer), Edna Jones (probationer), E. Pickens (assistant nurse), T. James (assistant nurse), V. Lane (probationer), J. Barnes (probationer). Front row: M. Griffiths (assistant nurse), G.M. Doughty (sister), Mrs E.A. Wills (matron), M. Roderick (sister), B. James (assistant nurse), Danny the dog.

Tynewydd Labour Club, Blaencwm room, six old club members. From left to right: Dai Davies (Kick), Shoni Parry, Dick Merry, -?- Thomas, Will Richards (Curly), Albert Hambury.

Boys from the RAFA Club. Rear from left to right: Jack Watkins, Gwyn Davies, Dai Morgan. Front: Tom Hughes, Des Jones, Eifion Williams.

Opposite above: Moonshiners Club, 1928-30.

Opposite below: Floral float in Miners Parade, 1984.

Jazz Band marching past the Treorchy Hotel during the miners' strike parade.

Desmond Dutfield speaking to the crowd in Cae Mawr field during the miners' strike parade.

Arthur Scargill gives his speech to the crowd in Cae Mawr field, Treorchy.

Miners and supporters.

Miners and supporters in Cae Mawr field, Treorchy.

Miners' strike parade passing through High Street, Treorchy, 1984.

Supporters from Reading branch Trade Union marching through High Street, Treorchy in 1984.

Supporters from Cwm Llantwit Lodge miners' parade. 1984.

Float leaving Penyrenglyn to join the miners' strike parade, 1984.

Miners' rally marching through Tynewydd, 1984. Extreme left: George Rees, Harry Pearce, Mal Phillips, Russel Wilks, -?- Jacka.

From left to right: George Rees, Arthur Scargill and Des Dutfield marching through Bute Street, Treorchy, 1984.

Maindy & Eastern Ambulance Force, *c.* 1910.

Ladies of Maes yr Haf Treherbert outing. In the picture are Mrs Evans, Mrs Thatcher, Mrs Powell and Lyn Basset.

St John's Ambulance volunteers on duty in Cae Mawr field, Treorchy, during the miners' strike.

Workers building the reservoir tunnel from Fernhill to the Llyn.

OPERA HOUSE

TREHERBERT.

THRS., FRI. and SAT., MAY 8, 9 and 10, 1924

Three Grand Performances of

THE

Will be given by the

∴ LIBANUS ∴ SUNDAY SCHOOL CHOIR

Conductor - Mr. Dillwyn Jones

Assisted by an

EFFICIENT ORCHESTRA

DRAMATIS PERSONÆ :

Laila - -	Miss Lizzie Francis
Fairy Queen -	Miss Jennie Rees
Beggar Mother -	Miss Jennie Rees
Mountain Child -	Miss Evelyn Eggarty

Chorus of Mountain Children, Fairies, &c.

Scene 1 -	-	A Grove on a Hillside
Scene 2	-	A Dark Gloomy Forest
Scene 3 -	-	A Grove on a Hillside

Accompanist -	-	MADAM MAY OWEN
Stage Manager	-	MR. DAVID JONES

Each Performance will be preceded by ACTION SONGS.

POPULAR PRICES :

Reserved (Numbered)	Back of Pit	Gallery
2s. & 1s. 6d.	1s.	6d.

Doors open at 6.30 ; to commence at 7 prompt.

Proceeds for Sunday School Funds.

Seats may be booked with the Secretary---Mr. T. J. Jones, 28 Dumfries Street, Treherbert

I JONES, PRINTER, TREHERBERT

Opera House poster.

six

Residents

Above: William Jenkins taking over presidency of Rotaract (Junior Rotary Club) from outgoing president, Barrie Davies, *c.*1982.

Below: From left to right: Norman Martin, Haydn Curtiss, Albert Nicholas (Alby Nick), Peter Jones.

Above: We are from the Town. Back row, from left to right: Gwyn Owen, Les Jones, Stan Eddy. Front row: Marjorie Jones, Des Howells, Margaret Davies.

Below: Alby and Myra Oliver living the dream, on holiday in Blackpool.

Above: Tynewydd Labour Club dance hall refreshment table, *c.* 1950. From left to right: Kitty Scott, Mary Evans, Rose Crane, Will Scott.

Ladies of Blaenrhondda.

Above: Young boys bathing in the brook near Nant Ffernol, Treherbert, *c.* 1915.

Opposite below: Men of Tynewydd village. Back row, from left to right: Jim Hanbury, Ieuen Watkins, Glan Evans, Meurig Thomas. Front row: Alan Evans, Norman Evans, Ieuen Lazarus. Alan and Norman Evans were brothers; Alan was killed in a motor accident during the Second World War and Norman was lost at sea.

Mr James sitting below falls bach, Cwmparc, *c.* 1927.

Group of ladies from Penyrenglyn.

Above: Fernhill Boys. In the back: Alan Stanton.
Middle row, from left to right: Johnney Jones,
Arthur John Davies, George Rees, Phillip Rees.
Front row: Danny Morgans, Graham Phillips
(Tiger), arms around Dai Rees, Glan Davies.

Right: Brothers George (left) and John Rowsell
(right).

Pickens Brothers, *c.* 1916. Back row, from left to right: James, Samuel. Phillip, Abraham (auctioneer). Front row: Robert, William (nephew from Australia), William.

Opposite above: Joseph Jones and family, *c.* 1910.

Opposite below: This photograph was taken in 1890. Father Pickens was born in 1837 and died in 1894. He lost his right leg in a tin mine in Cornwall. He became a tailor and made all the clothes you see in the picture. Back row, from left to right: James, Robert, John, Abraham. Front row: Samuel, Phillip, father Pickens, George, Caroline, William. There were two daughters, Annie and Ethel, who had emigrated to Australia. Samuel was the first man to die in Treherbert Hospital following a colliery accident.

From left to right: Edward Willey (1891–1912) drowned on the *Titanic*, his body was never recovered, Richard Willey (1865–1936), James Willey (1892–1965). Edward left the Rhondda aged three to be brought up by his grandparents in England. He had returned home to the Rhondda (when this photograph was taken) to obtain permission from his father Richard to emigrate to America to join his older brother.

Rhoda Willey family, No. 29 Mill Street, Ystrad, *c.* 1914. Back row, from left to right: Eva (1896–1930), mother Rhoda (1869–1943), Melinda (1897–1923), Ada (1900–1935). Front row: Ivy (1908–1925), Horace (1909–1988), Walter (1902–1972).

John Jones family of No. 12 Stanley Road, Gelli, *c.* 1898. From left to right: son Edgar, mother Gwen, baby Daisy, father John, daughter Elizabeth, son David.

Young men from 'the Moel', Pentre, *c.* 1910. Standing on the left is David Evans.

Opposite above: Pickens family, Taff Street, Treherbert, *c.* 1924. From left to right: Gladys, Trevor, Ethel. Sitting: William, Kate mother, Phillip father.

Opposite below: Unknown Blaencwm family, *c.* 1905.

Treherbert Railway canteen dance. In the photograph are Wilf Norman, Will Scott, Kitty Scott, Beryl Perkins and Ieuan Perkins.

Opposite above, left: Jean Taylor bangs the drum in the Herbert Street Carnival.

Opposite above, right: Hawaii girls, Herbert Street Carnival. Standing, from left to right: Pauline Tucker, Nicola Morris, Lynwen Jenkins, Michelle Collins. Kneeling: Alison Oliver, Maria Eynon.

Opposite below: Carol Oliver dressed as an Indian girl on horseback.

Blaencwm children in the park.

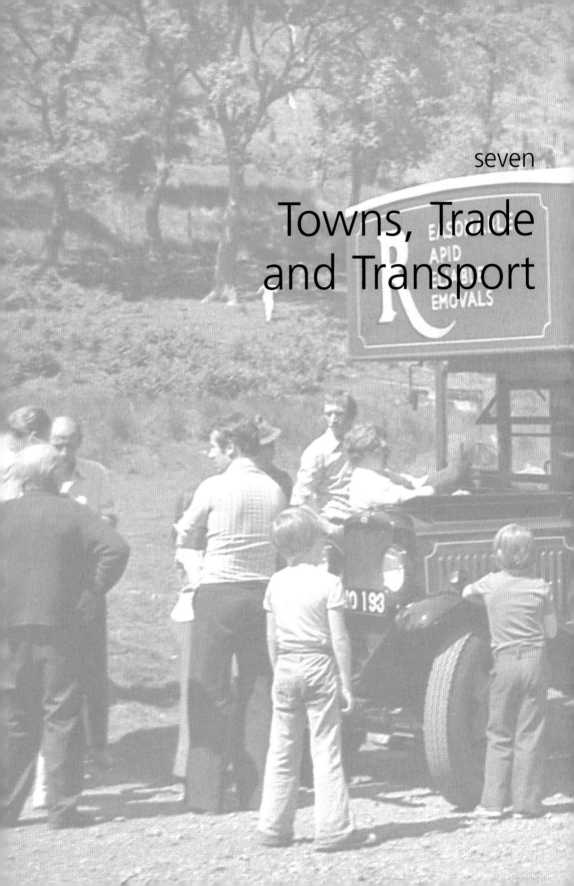

seven

Towns, Trade and Transport

Bute Street, Treherbert.

Gelli Colliery. The street on the mountain was known as 'Monkeys Tump'.

Fernhill houses decorated for Victory party.

Ystrad railway yard and station.

John Balestrazzi on the motorbike and sidecar from which he used to sell ice cream.

Vintage Nevline transport removal van ready to take part in the Tydraw Farm Riding School cavalcade, 1979.

Wyndham Rees's vintage 1929 Rolls Royce.

Balestrazzi ice-cream cart.

Alexandra pub, Treharne Street, Pentre.

Above: Railway Inn, Ystrad Road, *c.* 1910. Harry Chester was the proprietor.

Right: Edgars Newsagent, Gelli. Standing in the doorway: John Jones, Edgar's father and Lydia Jones, Edgar's wife.

The Direct Trading Co.

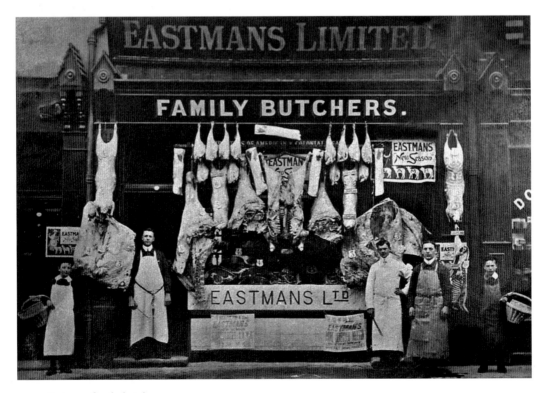

Eastmans family butchers.

Harry Powell, hairdresser, Dunraven Street, Treherbert, gives Dr Walter Williams a short back and sides, while another man waits for his turn. Shortly after this photograph was taken Harry closed shop and retired, leaving the contents and fittings to the National Folk Museum, St Fagans, Cardiff.

Turntable and railway sheds, Treherbert, c. 1938.

Above: 1919 Rover car outside Basini's Café, Treherbert.

Below: Ynysofeio Avenue charabanc trip arriving in Porthcawl. Front: Dickie, Maggie and Cliff Crabbe. Alby Oliver is behind in the middle of the three boys. The lady in the big flower pot hat is Mrs Crabbe and behind her is Mrs Drake. Mrs Greedy is peeking around the little boy in the striped scarf.

Right: A.L. Davies, No. 32 Wyndham Street, Tynewydd. It seems that the shop was run by Mrs Davies as her husband was a guard on the railway and the shop was known locally as 'Davies the Guard'. They had a daughter named Lizzie Joyce who played the organ in Ebenezer, taught music on the piano, gave voice training, and was the pianist for the Tynewydd Ladies' Choir in 1935.

Below: View of Cwmparc. Alice Boxhall Senior Citizens' Hall is in the foreground.

Llewellyn Street, Pentre. Siloh chapel on the right is undergoing demolition.

Stuart Hotel, Treherbert with Dunraven Street to the left and Abertonllwyd Street to the right and Pen Pych in the background, *c.* 1916.

Treherbert police station built in 1865. The picture was taken prior to its demolition on 27 March 1967.

View of Blaencwm from the top of Penpych Mountain.

Fernhill Workmans Hall, the Palace Cinema, Tynewydd, with Penpych Mountain in the background, *c.* 1940.

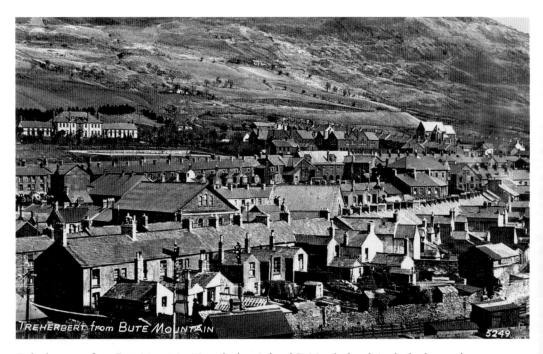

Treherbert seen from Bute Mountain. Note the hospital and St Mary's church in the background, *c.* 1932.

eight

Boy Lost on the Mountain

THIS PLAQUE MARKS THE SPOT
WHERE THE BODY OF
WILLY LLEWELLYN, AGED 5, WAS
FOUND. HE WAS LOST AT ABERAMAN
ON THE AFTERNOON OF APRIL 11TH
1902. WORK CEASED AT LOCAL PITS
AND AFTER A SEARCH BY THE
WHOLE COMMUNITY HIS
REMAINS WERE DISCOVERED ON
APRIL 26TH. HE IS BURIED AT
CEFN CEMETERY

MAE'R PLAC HWN YN COFNODI'R
MAN LLE DARGANFUWYD CORFF
WILLY LLEWELLYN, 5 MLWYDD
OED. AETH AR GOLL YN ABERAMAN
AR BRYNHAWN EBRILL 11EG 1902.
RHODDWYD Y GORAU I WEITHIO YN
Y PYLLAU LLEOL AC WEDI I'R
GYMUNED GYFAN YMUNO YN Y
CHWILIO DAETHPWYD O HYD I'W
WEDDILLION AR EBRILL 26AIN.
FE'I CLADDWYD YM MYNWENT CEFN

Mountain memorial, to a child named Willy Llewellyn, aged five. The following is a transcript from Owen 'Morien' Morgan's book *History of Pontypridd and Rhondda Valleys* published in 1903:

On the eleventh of April, 1902, a child named Willie Llywelin, five years of age accompanied his mother from home – No. 100, Heolgerrig, Merthyr – in a cart to Aberaman. She had gone shopping, and he disappeared unobserved from the shop. His mother hurried out and made every search for him in vain. It was later ascertained he had been in a sweet shop opposite, had then followed a cart up to Wind Street, Aberdare, a mile up the valley, then all trace of him was lost. A Mrs Reynolds reported that a boy answering his description, had at the foot of the Western mountains, called at her house for a drink of water. His parents lived beyond the Eastern range of mountains. In a few days the whole country was roused, and even London newspapers published every scrap of information obtainable touching the missing little one. All the collieries in the Aberdare Valley stopped, and one day it was estimated that 12,000 men were scouring the mountains in search of the little fellow. It was said he was a most intelligent child, and in the previous Easter Monday literary meeting connected with the chapel where his parents attended he had, by his recitation of two Welsh hymns, defeated all comers. On April 26th, his dead body was discovered on the heights of Blaen Rhondda, at a spot known as Caer Moesau, 300 yards to the west of the lofty Cairn, indicating the highest point in Glamorgan, 1,971 feet above the level of the Severn. He was found by Alderman William Morgan, J.P.,

Tynewydd, and Mr. John Morgan his son, and two others. On the Monday, two days later, the writer accompanied Mr John Morgan, on horseback, to the spot. It is 20 yards above the traces of the ancient parish road over the mountains towards the valleys in the direction of Glyncorrwg. From there, with an opera glass, one could see the route the child had walked after reaching the top of the mountains from Aberdare. He had walked a distance of about eight miles from Aberaman, and, as regards the mountains, they are about the least frequented in Glamorganshire. He had evidently attempted to go home before his mother, probably in a huff. He was found in his shirt sleeves. His under coat was laying a yard and a half from him, and his little overcoat had apparently been blown by the strong wind about twelve yards beyond him. It is conjectured that while seeing mountains rising in front of him, he thought his home was on the other side of them: that when he reached the dip of the mountains beyond, and beholding far below, to him unknown deep valleys, he, dead tired, sat down after taking off and wrapping his overcoat round his little head, the wind and cold being very keen there. That he slept there until some time in the dark morning, then awoke, and found himself alone and dripping wet. Then he took off his under coat, and lay down again now on his left arm under his head – that was the position he was found – and terror, exposure, and fatigue, ended his life before morning.

The following Saturday, April 30th, his funeral took place at Cefn Coed y Cymmer Cemetery. The public were so intensely sympathetic, that the concourse escorting the little remains was enormous, the throng, all in deepest mourning, occupying forty minutes in passing a given point.

Willy Llewellyn memorial marking the spot where his body was found placed here by the Rhondda Civic Historic Society in 2005. The inscription reads:

This plaque marks the spot where the body of Willy Llewellyn, aged 5 was found, he was lost at Aberaman on the afternoon of April 11th 1902. Work ceased at local pits and after a search by the whole community his remains were discovered on April 26th. He is Buried at Cefn cemetery.

It is also written in the Welsh language.

Other local titles published by Tempus

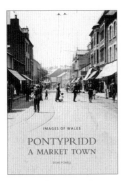

Pontypridd A Market Town

DEAN POWELL

Compiled with 200 images, this selection highlights some of the changes and events that have taken place in the South Wales market town of Pontypridd. From glimpses of heavy industry, including the Ynysangharad Works and surrounding collieries, to the arrival of the first electric tram to Pontypridd in March 1905, all aspects of working and social life are chronicled here. Aspects of everyday life are also recalled, from shops and pubs, places of worship and public buildings, to celebrations and local sporting heroes.

0 7524 3578 7

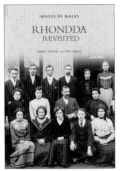

Rhondda Revisited

EMRYS JENKINS AND ROY GREEN

This collection of over 200 postcards and photographs, many never before published, highlights some of the important people who have populated, and places that have shaped, this important region of South Wales. Accompanied by supporting text, this book is a valuable pictorial addition to the histories of the area, which will reawaken nostalgic memories for some while offering a unique glimpse of the past for others.

0 7524 3388 1

Upper Rhondda Treorchy and Treherbert

EMRYS JENKINS AND ROY GREEN

Using images captured by the camera lens over the last 100 years, the authors have reconstructed the broad canvas of past life in the Upper Rhondda Fawr Valley. The selection is wide-ranging: from colliers to carnivals, soup kitchens to champion gardeners, hospital queens to blacksmiths. It will be of particular interest to those who have left the valley but still retain a love for their homeland.

0 7524 1016 4

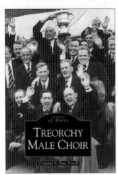

Treorchy Male Choir

DEAN POWELL

The history of Rhondda's world-renowned Treorchy Male Choir is rich in the diverse features of Welsh valley life. That history is lavishly documented in this volume of with over 200 photographs, cuttings and choir memorabilia from former members and admirers who enjoy their performances and recordings. It will delight the many who are fortunate to know the choir, and will also illustrate the fact that it is more than just a choir, but a 'way of life'.

0 7524 2238 3

If you are interested in purchasing other books published by Tempus, or in case you have difficulty finding any Tempus books in your local bookshop, you can also place orders directly through our website

www.tempus-publishing.com